KW-054-818

CONTENTS

ANIMATION

For thousands of years storytellers, poets and authors have used pictures to bring their tales to life. No one knows who was the first person to try to make the pictures move, but it was probably a Stone Age artist.

Look carefully at this cave painting. Doesn't it look as if the painter was trying to show the animals moving?

Perhaps ancient storytellers made moving shadow pictures in the firelight, too.

These shadow puppets are from Indonesia. They are used to tell the ancient stories of the *Ramayana* – the Hindu stories about Rama, his wife Sita, and their adventures in the land of the monkey god Hanuman.

The puppeteers work the puppets behind a screen onto which a bright light is shone, making moving pictures.

The rules are simple. Take your work, but never yourself, seriously. Pour in the love and whatever skill you have, and it will come out.
Chuck Jones, animator

Nowadays we can use cameras and computers to create animated films which make pictures move and puppets come alive.

In this book you'll be looking at how animators have used drawings and puppets to tell stories and you'll find out about some of the stars – human and animal – of animated films.

TWO PIONEER ANIMATORS

Eadweard Muybridge

Eadweard Muybridge was a British photographer and inventor who lived in the United States of America. He was fascinated by how animals move.

In 1878, before the first movie camera was invented, Muybridge found a way to photograph every movement of a galloping horse. He placed 50 cameras alongside a race track. Each camera was controlled by a string stretched across the track. As the horse galloped by, its hooves caught the strings. Each camera took a slightly different picture of the galloping horse, so every small movement of the horse was photographed.

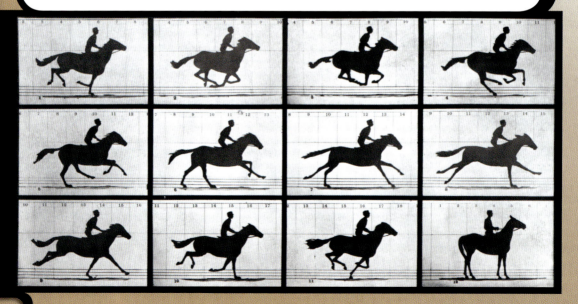

By photographing a falling cat, he also proved that cats can turn in the air and land on their feet.

Muybridge invented the zoopraxiscope, a very simple projector, to make his pictures move.

Muybridge printed his pictures on to a glass disc.

He put the glass disc into his zoopraxiscope. A light shone through as the disc was spun and the 'moving pictures' were projected onto a screen.

Winsor McCay

Winsor McCay began his career drawing comic strips. His most famous character was Little Nemo, a small boy who had fantastic adventures in his dreams.

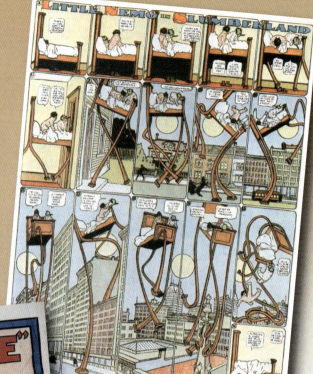

In 1911, McCay created the first animated animal star, Gertie the Dinosaur. Gertie was part of an act that McCay performed in theatres across the USA.

It was the first 'interactive' animation show.

McCay stood on the stage in front of a large screen. He called out 'Gertie!' and a cartoon dinosaur appeared on the screen. McCay then asked Gertie to do tricks, even catching an apple McCay pretended to throw to her.

Finally, McCay announced that Gertie would give him a ride. He walked behind the screen at the very moment that a cartoon McCay appeared on the screen. Gertie 'lifted' the cartoon McCay on to her back and they exited to enormous applause.

In 1914, McCay made a film in which he is seen drawing Gertie, who comes to life. McCay then steps into the cartoon himself, just like the stage show.

Animation is an extension of motion pictures, not an imitation. It should go where live action can't go.
Chuck Jones

ANIMAL CHARACTERS

People have always loved stories about animals, especially stories like *The Tortoise and the Hare* or the *Tales of Brer Rabbit*. These stories are about animals with human emotions: anger, pride, jealousy or love.

Since the first animated films like *Gertie the Dinosaur*, some of the most popular cartoon characters have been animals.

Felix the Cat was a big star in the early days of silent cinema, before sound was added to films. He was as popular as human film stars like Charlie Chaplin and Buster Keaton. People queued outside cinemas for hours to see a Felix cartoon. Felix was also the star of the first experimental TV broadcasts in New York in 1928.

However, like a lot of silent stars' films, Felix's talking films weren't popular. The public went crazy for a new 'talking' cartoon star: Mickey Mouse. (It wasn't the last time a cartoon cat was beaten by a cartoon mouse!) Today, Felix is popular again, starring in computer games and online comics.

When people laugh at Mickey Mouse, it's because he's so human; and that is the secret of his popularity... There's nothing funnier than the human animal.
Walt Disney

Tom and Jerry

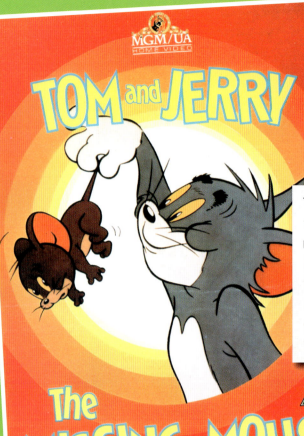

Tom and Jerry are a cartoon double act, based on human slapstick comedy acts like Laurel and Hardy.

Tom is a cat who is always trying to catch Jerry the mouse. Jerry sets elaborate booby traps for Tom. In every film poor Tom gets hit with a variety of things, from garden rakes and cooking pots to ten tonne weights.

Bugs Bunny

Bugs Bunny, like Brer Rabbit or Anansi, is always playing tricks on bigger or more dangerous characters. Bugs's main enemy is Elmer Fudd, a hunter. In many of the films, Elmer is trying to shoot Bugs, while Bugs plays a variety of tricks on Elmer which often involve Bugs dressing up in elaborate disguises.

I have to think as Bugs Bunny, not of Bugs Bunny. I let the part of me that is Bugs come to the surface, knowing, with regret, that I can never match his marvellous confidence.
Chuck Jones, co-creator of Bugs Bunny

HAND DRAWN ANIMATION

If you look at a piece of cine-film very closely, you'll see it's made up of thousands of tiny photographs, each slightly different.

Animated films are made in the same way, with lots of tiny pictures all slightly different – but these pictures have to be drawn first.

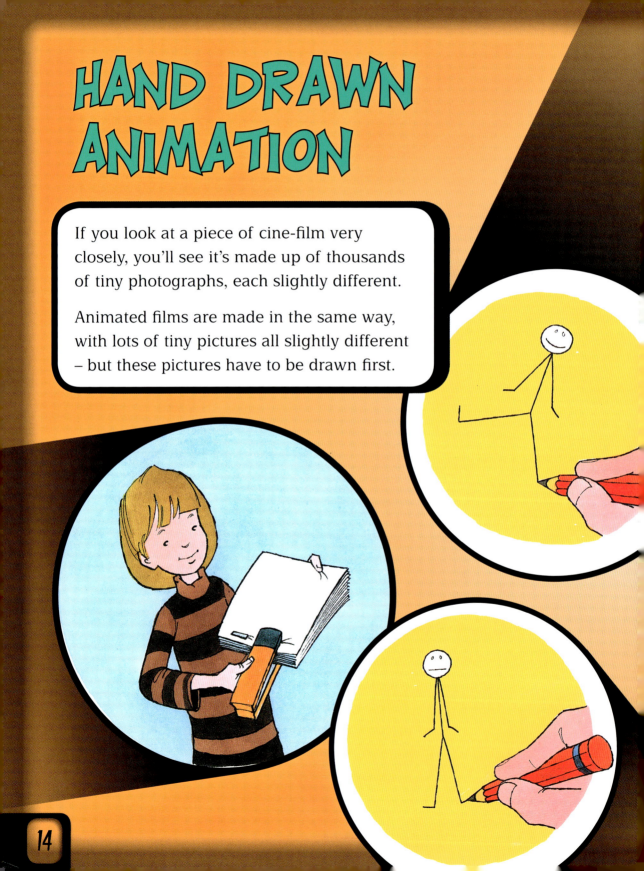

Make your own simple animation

You will need:

- a few sheets of paper, approximately 10 cm x 10 cm
- a stapler
- a pencil or pen
- or instead of the sheets of paper use a small notebook

1. If you're not using a notebook, staple the paper together along one edge to make a book.
2. Draw a simple matchstick person on the last page.
3. Turn the page. On the new page, trace the figure you have drawn, but make a small change in the drawing so one of the arms or legs is in a slightly different position.
4. Repeat stage 3 over the next few pages, each time making small changes to your person's arms or legs from the previous drawing.
5. Flick the pages with your thumb from back to front and watch your cartoon person move.

15

CLAYMATION

A close shave for Gromit the dog during the filming of a *Wallace and Gromit* adventure.

Many of the most successful modern animated films use puppets made of clay or Plasticine™, instead of drawings. This is called claymation.

It works in a similar way to drawn animation. A clay puppet is photographed, then moved very slightly and photographed again and again and again. Like drawn animation at least 12 pictures are needed for one second of film.

Morph first appeared in 1978 on *Take Hart* – a BBC TV art series for children. He lived in a wooden box on the desk of Tony Hart, the presenter. Every week Morph got into trouble, tripping over pencils, falling into bottles of ink or knocking over pots of paint in Tony's studio.

Morph was short-tempered, rather pompous and a show-off – all rather negative things, but oddly enough they made him seem attractive.
Peter Lord, co-creator of Morph

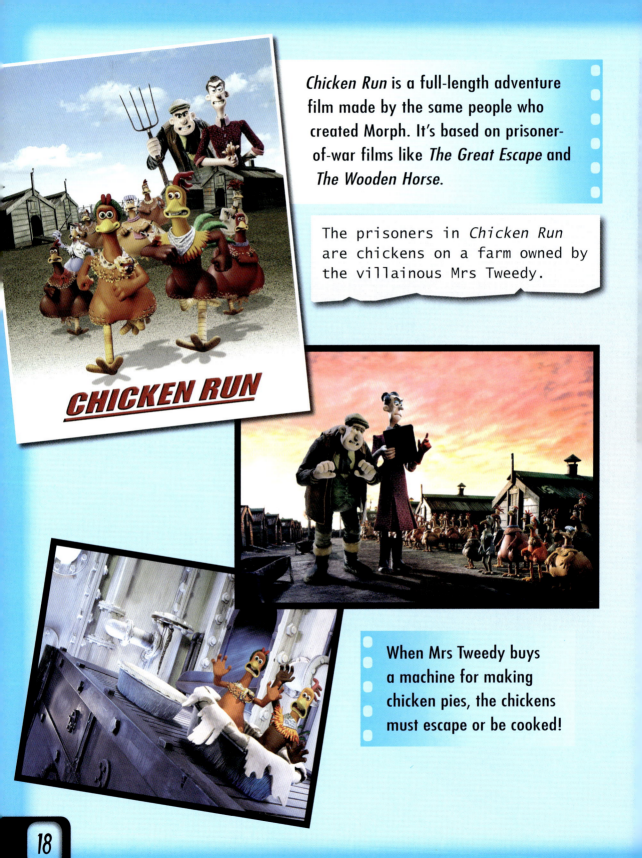

Chicken Run is a full-length adventure film made by the same people who created Morph. It's based on prisoner-of-war films like *The Great Escape* and *The Wooden Horse*.

The prisoners in *Chicken Run* are chickens on a farm owned by the villainous Mrs Tweedy.

CHICKEN RUN

When Mrs Tweedy buys a machine for making chicken pies, the chickens must escape or be cooked!

Nick Park, co-director of *Chicken Run*, is filming Mr and Mrs Tweedy with the horrible new machine for making pies.

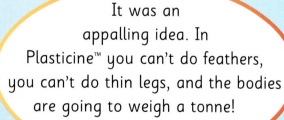

When we first discussed the idea for *Chicken Run*, Pete's reaction was pure horror.
Nick Park

It was an appalling idea. In Plasticine™ you can't do feathers, you can't do thin legs, and the bodies are going to weigh a tonne!
Peter Lord

STOP MOTION

Make your own claymation

Morph was just a ball of clay that could take on any shape,
so you could start by making your own Morph.

You will need:

- a computer
- a camera — it could be a camcorder or a web cam
- a tripod to keep the camera still
- software, like iStopMotion if you've got an Apple computer, or Stop Motion Maker or Stop Motion Pro if you're using a PC
- ball of clay

1 Place your camera on a tripod (it's important that the camera doesn't move). Focus the camera on a small, well-lit, flat surface.

2 Place a ball of clay on the surface. Switch on your computer and start the software. Your software will control the camera. You'll see the picture in a 'viewfinder' and there'll be a 'button' to click on to take the picture.

3 | Take your first picture.

4 | Change the shape of the clay very slightly. Your software should show you a faint impression of your last picture. This is called 'onion-skinning'. It helps you check that your next picture will fit the sequence. Take your second picture.

5 | Repeat step 4, gradually turning the clay into the shape of a person.

Lewi Firth Bolton, an animator from Bridlington, sent his latest film to Nick Park and Peter Lord. They were so impressed they offered him a job, but Lewi couldn't accept it because he was only 14. Lewi makes all his films in his bedroom, using an ordinary digital camera and a computer!

REVENGE OF THE DINOSAURS!

In 1991, the director Steven Spielberg began making a film where dinosaurs and people would once again appear together, as they did in McCay's film about Gertie.

In *Jurassic Park* there is no apple catching or circus tricks: these dinosaurs are angry and dangerous!

I've been interested in dinosaurs since I was a child. A Harvard **psychiatrist** was asked why kids love dinosaurs so much. He said, 'That's easy. They're big, they're fierce… and they're dead.'
Steven Spielberg, director of *Jurassic Park*

Many of the dinosaurs were animated by computers. The computers created 'digital puppets' on screen which could be added to the film later.

The actors were told where the dinosaurs would be, and then had to imagine the dinosaurs were there when acting a scene.

Ariana Richards, who played Lex, one of the two children in the film, remembers watching the finished film after the dinosaurs had been added to the scenes: 'I was blown away! Scenes where there hadn't been dinosaurs before – like the one where they're stampeding in a field – it was breathtaking…. I actually got scared watching it, even though I'd been on the set.'

That's all folks!
Bugs Bunny

Filmography

Chicken Run, Pathe, directed by Peter Lord and Nick Park, voices by Julia Sawahla, Jane Horrocks, Mel Gibson and others.

Fantasia (1941), Walt Disney.

Gertie the Dinosaur (1914), directed by Winsor McCay, available to download from Google Video.

Jurassic Park (1993), Universal Pictures Video, directed by Steve Spielberg and starring Sam Neill, Laura Dern and Jeff Goldblum.

Looney Tunes Golden Collection Volume 2, Warner Home Video. 4 CD set of Bugs Bunny, Daffy Duck, Porky Pig, Road Runner, many directed by Chuck Jones, including What's Opera, Doc?

Snow White and the Seven Dwarfs (1937), Walt Disney.

Tom and Jerry Classic Collection Volume 2, Warner Home Video

Toy Story, Walt Disney Home Video, voices by Tim Allen and Tom Hanks and others.

Wallace and Gromit: Three Cracking Adventures, 2 Entertain Video, directed by Nick Park, voices by Peter Sallis and others.

Further details of software

For Macs: iStopmotion further information & downloads from www.boinx.com including information on special support for schools and teachers through Curriculum Online

For PC: Stopmotionmaker further information and downloads, both full versions and trials: www.stopmotionmaker.com

Stop Motion Pro: further details & downloads www.stopmotionpro.com including information on special support for teachers and schools through Curriculum Online

Index